Financial Independence

Your Guide to a Richer Life

Table of Contents

Chapter 1. Introduction

Discover the path to financial independence with our comprehensive Special Report, "Financial Independence: Your Guide to a Richer Life". Free yourself from the chains of financial uncertainty as we facilitate a transformative journey to self-sufficiency. Our easy-to-understand guide will intricately break down the complexities of personal finance, helping pave your way towards a future exuding financial confidence. Whether you're a seasoned investor or a beginner just dipping your toes into the world of finance, our invigorating report is designed to foster a sense of empowerment, encouraging you to control your financial destiny. Secure your financial future today – and live a richer, more fulfilling life tomorrow. Buckle up, and let this guide steer you into the fast lane on the road to financial independence.

Chapter 2. Understanding Financial Independence

Understanding financial independence is the first step to achieving it. This paradigm-shift requires both a solid comprehension of the concept and its cardinal constituents, and the cultivation of a mindset conducive to leading a financially autonomous life.

2.1. The Essence of Financial Independence

Financial independence is a state in which your wealth works for you instead of you toiling for it. It implies possessing ample resources or savings capable of covering your living expenses for an indefinite period, eliminating the requirement to be actively involved in a job or business to earn money. It provides the freedom to fully pursue your passions and interests, rather than putting them on the backburner for survival.

Attaining financial independence doesn't automatically denote leading a life of lavishness; it merely signifies achieving a position where finances aren't a cause of stress or an impediment to living life on your terms.

Intrinsic to this pursuit is the process of learning to control your money, as opposed to letting it control you. It challenges traditional concepts of earning and spending by promoting intelligent investment, reasonable saving, and conscious consumption.

2.2. Factors Influencing Financial Independence

Several factors contribute to one's journey towards financial independence. These include your financial planning, current income level, investment strategy, expenditure model, market conditions, and the timeframe within which you aim to achieve this goal. Let's discuss these factors in detail:

2.2.1. Income

Typically, those with higher income levels can potentially achieve financial independence sooner, given more funds to invest; however, income is just one factor. Economic self-sufficiency can be accrued at almost any income level, as it primarily hinges on how much of that income is saved and invested effectively.

2.2.2. Expenses

The key to financial independence isn't solely about earning more, but also about learning to live below your means. This entails maintaining a living standard proportionate to or lower than income level, not the credit limit. By decreasing expenses, you increase your savings potential, accelerating the path to financial independence.

2.2.3. Investments

Investing is indispensable for achieving financial independence. By introducing your savings to the right investment opportunities, you enable your money to grow over time. Assorted investment avenues, such as mutual funds, stocks, bonds, real estate, etc., cater to different risk appetites, return expectations, and investment durations, providing you with multiple routes to financial freedom.

2.2.4. Time

The timeframe within which you attain financial independence is contingent on your savings ratio, return on investments, and the age at which you begin saving and investing. The earlier you start, the more time your money has to grow and compound, pivoting you closer to your goal.

2.3. Financial Independence Ratio

The Financial Independence Ratio (FIR) provides a measure of your journey towards financial autonomy. It's computed by dividing your passive income by your expenses. Passive income includes returns from investments, rental income, and any other income sources that require minimal active participation.

If your FIR is less than 1, you're financially dependent. If your FIR equals 1, you've achieved financial sustainability, where your passive income equals your expenses. If your FIR exceeds 1, congratulations, you've achieved financial independence, as your passive income outstrips your living costs.

Financial independence isn't a dream exclusive to the rich and famous. It's a feasible reality for anyone equipped with discipline, determination, and right financial knowledge. The next few pages delve deeper into the financial adeptness requisite for this journey - conceiving a strategy, cultivating the right mindset, embracing frugality, and making smart investment choices. You'll soon realize that your quest for financial independence is a marathon, not a sprint, and every little step counts! Let's move forward to the detailed strategies for achieving this auspicious principle, ensuring a future as rewarding as it is financially secure.

(Continued on next page...)

Chapter 3. Defining Your Financial Goals

Time and again, the question has been asked, "What is the first step towards achieving financial independence?" To this, the answer has been unwavering and unanimously agreed upon: defining your financial goals is the foremost priority.

3.1. Understanding the Importance of Financial Goals

To set off on a journey, one must first know their destination. Similarly, your financial journey must begin with clear, well-defined goals. Goals keep you focused, driven, and they provide an endpoint to measure your progress against. A ship without a rudder drifts aimlessly, and so will your financial journey without well-defined goals. Identifying life ambitions, consolidating current financial standing, and setting clear, achievable financial milestones can elevate your journey from being a random walk towards becoming a purposeful expedition.

3.2. Identifying Your Financial Goals

When you begin to delineate your financial aspirations, consider both the short-term and long-term scope of your life. Short-term goals could include saving for a new car, taking a vacation, or paying off a particular debt. Long-term goals might include securing a comfortable retirement, funding a child's education, or owning a home.

Here, use the SMART (Specific, Measurable, Achievable, Relevant, Time-bound) goal-setting method. This proven approach provides a clearly structured pathway to achieving your financial objectives. Write down your goals. Putting them down on paper adds a level of commitment and makes your goals seem more attainable.

Let's apply the SMART framework:

- **Specific:** Be precise about what you want to achieve, like "I want to save $10,000 for my postgraduate degree."

- **Measurable:** You should be able to track your progress. A measurable goal could be "I want to save $200 every month."

- **Achievable:** The goal should be realistic, considering your income and financial commitments, "I can cut down on dining out to $50 per month to help achieve this goal."

- **Relevant:** Ensure that your objectives align with your life goals or overall plan. If your main aim is financial independence, then a goal like "buying a luxurious car" may not be relevant.

- **Time-bound:** Assign a time frame to your goal. "I want to save $10,000 for my postgraduate degree in the next 5 years" prompts you to act promptly.

3.3. Classification of Financial Goals

Having a time frame for your financial goals also helps categorize them into short-term, mid-term, and long-term objectives:

- **Short-term goals (1-3 years):** These goals can include saving for vacation, building an emergency fund, paying off a small debt, etc.

- **Mid-term goals (4-7 years):** Mid-term goals could include saving for a down payment on a house, paying off a significant debt, or accumulating funds for a business startup.

- **Long-term goals (7+ years):** These may be saving for your child's education, amassing a retirement fund, purchasing a home, and so forth.

3.4. Financial Goals and Budgeting

Once the goals are set, gear up your budget to pave the way. Design your budget around your financial goals. Align it towards proactively saving and investing to achieve these goals, rather than impulsively spending and then saving what's left – if there's anything left at all. This shift in mindset creates a proactive financial management approach.

3.5. Prioritization of Financial Goals

Not all goals carry equal weight. Some might be essential for your future financial security (like saving for retirement), while others could be more about improving your quality of life (like going on a dream vacation). The key is to strike a balance between the two and prioritize accordingly.

3.6. Review and Revising Your Financial Goals

Setting your financial goals is not a one-time exercise. As your life circumstances change - marriage, children, change in occupation, etc., - so may your financial goals. Regularly revisit your goals to ensure they are still relevant and adjust if needed.

Remember, it is not about reaching your final financial destination overnight. It's about embarking on a journey towards financial independence, one achievable goal at a time. As you set sail, keep this guide at hand, redefine your goals as needed, and navigate your financial journey at your own pace.

Chapter 4. The Art of Budgeting and Saving

Understanding, and prudently managing your cash flow is the foundation of achieving financial independence. In simpler terms, the cornerstone of financial self-sustainability lies in creating a sound budget and developing the discipline to abide by it. The path to financial independence can be an exhilarating yet challenging one, but by harnessing the power of budgeting and saving, you can transform financial uncertainty into opportunity. Let's delve into the intricate art of budgeting and saving.

4.1. Step 1: Understand where your money goes

The first, and arguably, the most critical step in the budgeting process is gaining comprehension of your monetary inflows and outflows. Begin by calculating your net income – your take-home pay after taxes and other deductions. Bear in mind to consider all your income sources including wages, pensions, government benefits, investment income, and even sporadic incomes such as bonuses or gifts.

Next, track your monthly expenditure. This usually encompasses both fixed and variable expenses. Fixed expenses are those that don't deviate much each month, such as mortgage or rental payments, utilities, insurance, and subscriptions. On the other hand, variable expenses fluctuate monthly and can include food, clothing, entertainment, and personal care.

4.2. Step 2: Create a Basic Budget Plan

Upon understanding your income and expense structure, you'll need to create your budget. One prevalent and recommended approach is the 50/30/20 rule of budgeting, where you partition your net income into three distinct categories: * 50% for needs: These are your non-negotiable expenses such as food, housing, utilities, and health insurance. * 30% for wants: This portion can be used for discretionary expenses including dining out, hobbies, and non-essential goods. * 20% for savings: This segment should be allocated towards savings and debt repayment.

Be sure to fine-tune this framework by considering your personal financial circumstances and goals.

4.3. Step 3: Monitor your Budget and Make Necessary Adjustments

The strength of a budget lies in its accurate reflection of your financial life. As your financial circumstances evolve, it becomes imperative to consistently monitor and adjust your budget accordingly. Moreover, don't forget to factor in irregular expenses such as gifts, holidays, or one-off medical costs.

4.4. Savings: The Vehicle to Financial Independence

While budgeting helps control your spending and increases your self-awareness about your financial habits, savings is the vehicle that gets you to the destination of financial independence. Unfortunately, there isn't a one-size-fits-all approach for savings. Much depends on your financial goals and personal circumstances. However, to help you kick-start your savings, we outline below some effective strategies.

4.5. Step 1: Build an Emergency Fund

An emergency fund acts as a financial buffer against unexpected events, such as job loss, health emergencies, or unexpected repairs. Ideally, your emergency fund should have enough to cover three to six months' worth of living expenses.

4.6. Step 2: Set Financial Goals

Once your emergency fund is robust, start setting financial goals. This could be anything from saving for a vacation, making a home down payment, or even retiring at a certain age. By knowing what you're saving for, you'll be more motivated to save.

4.7. Step 3: Prioritize and Automate your Savings

Make saving money a non-negotiable by treating it as a bill that needs to be paid. Automate savings wherever possible to remove the element of choice. For instance, if you receive a paycheck, set up a direct deposit into a savings account.

4.8. Conclusion

Budgeting and saving are not just about restricting your spending or tucking money away for a rainy day. They are about empowering you to make the best use of your financial resources, aligning your financial habits with your values and goals, and ultimately, making your money work for you. The path to financial independence, while not without its challenges, can be rewarding and satisfying, and mastering the art of budgeting and saving is a step in the right direction.

Chapter 5. The Power of Compound Interest

Financial stability is an intricate weave of various components, but one thread that stands out, due to its easily overlooked yet incredibly impactful nature, is compound interest. Touted as the eighth wonder of the world by none other than Albert Einstein, compound interest is a critically successful tactic often used by savvy investors to grow their wealth. To understand the power and the potential of compound interest, it's vital to grasp what it is, how it works, and ways to make it work for you.

5.1. Understanding Compound Interest

The straightforward explanation of compound interest is that it's 'interest on interest.' When you invest or save money in a financial product offering compound interest, not only is interest calculated on the initial amount you deposited or invested (the principal), but also on the interest that the principal amount has already earned. This differs substantially from simple interest, which only earns interest on the principal amount.

Let's illustrate with an example. Suppose you invest $1000 at an annual interest rate of 5%. With simple interest, you will earn $50 at the end of the first year, making your total $1050. If the money remains invested, you will earn another $50 at the end of the second year, taking your total to $1100.

However, the story changes with compound interest. In the first year, just like the simple interest scenario, you'd earn $50, making your total $1050. In the second year, though, the interest is calculated on $1050, not the initial $1000. Therefore, you'd earn $52.5 in the second year, making the total at the end of two years $1102.5. This $2.5 difference may seem small, but compounding is a powerful tool in long-term investments, where these small additions can snowball into significant gains due to the magic of compounding.

5.2. The Factors Influencing Compound Interest

There are three fundamental factors that determine the profitability of compound interest: the principal amount, the rate of interest, and time.

The principal amount is simply the money you initially deposit or invest. Naturally, the larger the principal, the more interest you can generate.

The rate of interest is also tied directly to the amount of money you make. A higher interest rate means higher returns, but it's essential to remember that high rates often come hand in hand with higher risk.

Time is where the magic happens. The longer you hold your investment, the greater the compounding effect. Your money exponentially grows over time with compound interest, which is why it's a vital component in long-term investment strategies.

5.3. The Math Behind Compound Interest

The formula to calculate compound interest is:

$A = P (1 + r/n)^{(nt)}$

Where: A is the amount of money accumulated after n years,

including interest. P is the principal amount (the initial amount of money). r is the annual interest rate (in decimal). n is the number of times that interest is compounded per year. t is the time the money is invested for, in years.

The exponential part of this formula is critical, as it's the component that creates the compounding effect, leading to exponential growth instead of linear growth.

5.4. Compound Interest and Your Investment Strategy

Understanding compound interest is key to creating a robust investment strategy. A preference for compound interest can greatly affect your choice of investment. Stock dividends, for example, can also benefit from compounding when you reinvest the dividend back into buying more stocks. The same principle applies to certain types of bonds and mutual funds.

Compound interest also rewards regular investments. By investing a fixed amount at regular intervals, you not only leverage market fluctuations via dollar-cost averaging, but you also enjoy compound growth on your investments. Over time, this can exponentially expand your portfolio.

5.5. Maximizing Compound Interest

Your best allies to maximize compound interest are time, rate of return, and regular investment. The earlier you start investing, the more time your investments have to grow. The higher the rate of return, the faster your money grows. Regular investments keep feeding the compounding machine, accelerating growth even more.

Remember, though. It's important to balance compounding growth with acceptable risk. High-return investments often carry substantial risks, which make them unsuitable for many investors. A balanced portfolio, combining high and low risk, can be a safer route to wealth accumulation.

Whether helping to make the most out of a savings account or becoming a cornerstone of a long-term investment plan, understanding the fundamental power of compound interest can literally pay dividends. Embrace the 'interest on interest' today and enjoy greater financial independence tomorrow.

Chapter 6. Investing Fundamentals: Stocks, Bonds, and More

Stemming from the desire to leverage your money to generate wealth, investing is an indispensable tool on the journey to financial independence. It involves purchasing assets such as stocks, bonds, mutual funds, real estate, or even starting your own business, with the hopes that the asset will generate income or appreciate in value over time. This chapter constitutes an in-depth exploration into the fundamental categories of investments.

=== Understanding the Roles of Stocks

In the financial market, stocks represent financial instruments that grant ownership rights over a company. When you buy a stock, you essentially buy a piece of that company. As a stockholder, you potentially derive a financial benefit in two primary ways; either through an increase in the stock's value or by receiving dividends, which are a portion of the company's profits distributed to its shareholders.

Investing in stocks carries potential high rewards due to their potential for significant growth. However, they also come with higher risk because if the company performs poorly or goes bankrupt, the value of your stock may decrease significantly or become worthless.

The key to successful stock investing lies within a balanced portfolio, time, patience, and a solid understanding of the companies you invest in. Consider diversifying your investment across various sectors and industries to protect yourself from the potential downfall of a single company or sector.

=== Delving into Bonds

Unlike stocks, bonds do not denote ownership. Rather, they signify a loan from the bondholder (investor) to the bond issuer, which can be a corporation or government. The bond issuer promises to pay the bondholder the face value of the bond upon its maturity, with periodic interest payments, known as coupon payments.

One of the primary advantages of bonds is the predictability they offer. Unless the issuer defaults, you'll receive your investment back along with the promised interest. This makes bonds an attractive option for conservative investors looking to preserve capital. However, the potential return on bonds is typically lower than that for stocks.

Diversification is key even within your bond investments. Consider incorporating a mix of different types of bonds in your portfolio like government bonds, corporate bonds, and municipal bonds, each carrying their own risk levels and returns.

=== Exploring Mutual Funds

A mutual fund pools money from multiple investors to invest in a diversified portfolio of stocks, bonds, or other assets, managed by professional fund managers.

The appeal of mutual funds lies in their inherent diversification, accessibility and professional management, making them an ideal choice for beginners. However, do be aware of potential fees and your comfort level with your investment decisions being managed by someone else.

=== The Real Estate Avenue

Real estate investments involve purchasing properties for rental purposes or for resale at a profit. These investments can be beneficial due to rental income, property value appreciation, and certain tax advantages. Still, real estate requires significant initial investment, continual property maintenance, dealing with tenants, understanding local market conditions, and could be subject to market fluctuations.

=== Starting Your Own Business

Starting a business can be a powerful wealth-generation tool. Though it requires a significant amount of effort and carries substantial risk, the financial and personal rewards potentially outweigh the risks if the business becomes successful.

Before jumping into this realm of investment, it's crucial to thoroughly research and develop a robust business plan. Consider seeking guidance from experienced entrepreneurs and professionals in your intended industry.

Investing can be a powerful vehicle towards financial independence, but it is not without risk. Hence, understanding the basics and diversifying your portfolio is paramount. Consider consulting with a financial advisor before making decisions. In all, remember that investing is not about getting rich quick, but about growing your wealth steadily over time with patience, diligence, and informed decision-making. Future chapters will delve into the strategies and tools at your disposal to optimize your investments for your financial independence journey.

Chapter 7. Navigating the Real Estate Market

Let us begin by demystifying the concepts of the real estate market, a pivotal driver for financial independence.

The real estate market consists of a multitude of investment opportunities, each with its own unique set of advantages and challenges. It includes residential, commercial, and industrial properties, as well as raw land ready for development. We will delve into the workings of these sectors, how to research potential investments, and how to leverage different strategies to yield a profit.

7.1. Exploring the Real Estate Sectors

Our foray into real estate starts with understanding its various sectors. Each sector has unique driving factors and market dynamics, necessitating careful planning and consideration before committing to an investment.

Residential real estate focuses on properties for individual or family residential use. It ranges from single-family homes to multi-story apartment complexes and everything in between. The value of residential real estate usually depends on factors like location, local amenities, and the condition of the property.

Commercial real estate primarily includes properties used for business purposes, like offices, retail spaces, or warehouses. The commercial property market generally hinges on economic factors at large—local business growth, employment rates, and consumer confidence can all significantly influence this sector.

Industrial real estate refers to properties specifically used for industrial business activities, including factories, warehouses, and distribution centers. Unlike residential and commercial properties, industrial real estate often depends on different factors, like proximity to transport hubs, utility access, and local zoning laws.

Finally, **land** refers to undeveloped properties without any construction done. It offers investors a blank canvas for development but generally necessitates considerable expertise and resources.

7.2. Understanding Real Estate Research

Purchasing properties, be it residential, commercial, industrial, or land, calls for meticulous research. This section will shed light on the art of research that precedes and guides every successful real estate investment.

Property Status and Condition: Start with evaluating the property's condition and any renovations needed. Inspections can reveal hidden costs that might impact the viability of your investment.

Neighborhood Analysis: Examine the neighborhood, focusing on aspects like schools, crime rate, nearby amenities, future development plans, and employment statistics. These factors often affect property values significantly.

Market Trends: Historical and expected future trends can influence real estate prices. Analyze data like historical sales prices, rent trends, vacancy rates, and supply-demand stats to develop an understanding of the market dynamics.

Local Laws and Regulations: Real estate law can be complex, revolving around state or even local legislation. Understand zoning laws, possible rent control regulations, and potential tax implications for any property you're considering.

7.3. Strategies for Real Estate Investment

Once you've carried out your research, it's time to turn to investment strategies. Each strategy carries different levels of risk, required expertise, and potential return on investment.

The most straightforward real estate investment strategy is **Buy and Hold**. Investors purchase a property and rent it out, providing them with a steady stream of rental income while the property hopefully appreciates in value over time.

House Hacking involves an investor living in their rental property and renting out rooms or units. It can reduce or even eliminate living expenses, making it a popular option for beginner investors.

Fix and Flip involves buying a property in need of renovations, renovating it, and reselling it at a higher price. The key to success lies in correctly estimating both renovation costs and the property's after-repair value.

Real Estate Wholesaling is when you contract with a property seller, find an interested buyer, and transfer the contract to them, earning money from the contract assignment fee.

REIT Investments offer the chance to invest in real estate without the need for property management. Real Estate Investment Trusts (REITs) are companies that own, operate, or finance real estate. Investors can buy shares of these businesses, much like buying stocks.

7.4. Mitigating Risks in Real Estate

Risk is inherent in any investment, and real estate is no exception. However, the danger can be minimized through careful planning, due diligence, and diversification.

Diversification: Your real estate portfolio should contain properties from different sectors and locations to protect against market fluctuations.

Insurance: Protect your investment from natural disasters, property damage, or accidents with insurance.

Negotiating Terms: Try to negotiate favorable terms in your contracts to minimize risks.

Financial Cushion: Build a financial cushion for unforeseen expenses like repairs, maintenance, and periods of vacancy.

7.5. Reaping the Rewards of Real Estate

After all the strategies implemented, risks mitigated, and sweat equity invested, the real reward is the steady stream of income generated and the potential for real estate appreciation. Rental income can provide cash flow, while property appreciation can build wealth over time. Moreover, tax advantages such as deductions and credits can increase your bottom line considerably.

The path to financial independence through the real estate market is not a quick sprint but a well-planned marathon. By understanding the unique characteristics and dynamics of the real estate market, you can carefully plot your course, navigate the challenges that arise, and ultimately achieve the financial independence you seek.

Chapter 8. Retirement Planning and Pension Schemes

Retirement can bring about mixed emotions. On one hand, it's the culmination of an enriching professional journey. On the other, it ushers in a period with no regular income. The thought of a paycheck-less future can unsettle even the best of us. However, strategic planning and diligent investments in pension schemes can see you through this phase comfortably.

8.1. The Importance of Retirement Planning

Retirement planning is one of the most critical components of personal finance. It helps safeguard your financial future by creating a steady flow of income, even in the absence of salaried employment. A sound retirement plan doesn't just offer financial security but provides the means to fulfill post-retirement dreams. Be it traveling around the globe, taking up a new hobby or volunteering for a cause close to your heart, a well-conceived retirement plan can make all these a reality.

Financial advisors often stress the need to start retirement planning early. The primary reason is time. The earlier you begin, the bigger your retirement fund, thanks to the compounding effect. A small investment made today can grow into a large nest egg over time, helping you achieve fiscal independence during your golden years.

8.2. Understanding Pension Schemes

Pension schemes are a popular retirement tool that provide a regular income to people post-retirement, ensuring financial security. Most pension schemes work on the fundamental principle of making regular contributions during a person's working life which then accumulate to provide a lump sum or steady income upon retirement.

Understanding the different types of pension schemes available can help you make an informed decision:

1. Defined Contribution Pension: This type of pension scheme is based on how much money you've paid into your pot and the growth of your investments. The retirement income itself is not guaranteed and is subject to market risks.

2. Defined Benefit Pension: These schemes promise a specific retirement income based on your earnings, tenure, and the age at which you retire. It's often seen as less risky for the individual.

3. State Pension: This is a pension you receive from the government upon retirement. While the amount is generally lesser than what you could get from workplace pensions, it provides a steady income.

8.3. Steps to Effective Retirement Planning

Regardless of your choice of pension scheme, an effective retirement plan follows a few basic steps.

1. Determine Your Retirement Needs: First and foremost, calculate how much income you'll require in retirement. Make allowances for inflation, healthcare costs, and lifestyle choices.

2. Start Saving Early: The sooner you begin to save, the larger your retirement fund due to compound interest.

3. Create a Diversified Portfolio: Don't rely on just your workplace pension; consider personal pensions, investments in stocks, bonds, and real estate to diversify your income streams.

4. Plan for Healthcare: With aging comes increased healthcare needs. Ensuring you have the right healthcare coverage will alleviate some financial stress.

5. Regularly Review and Adjust Your Plan: Life is unpredictable. It's important to review your retirement plan periodically and amend it as necessary.

8.4. How to Select the Right Pension Scheme

Selecting the right pension scheme may seem daunting due to the plethora of options available. When choosing your pension scheme, consider your risk tolerance, age, retirement goals, and the stability of the pension provider. A diverse portfolio is key to mitigating risks. An ideal portfolio would contain a mix of high-risk-high-return and low-risk-low-return investments. Financial advisors can provide assistance in creating a portfolio tailored to your needs.

8.5. Strategies for a Secure Retirement

Strategies like delaying your pension, purchasing an annuity, or investing in drawdown schemes can provide financial security in retirement.

1. Delaying Pension: By delaying your pension, you could potentially receive higher payments later.

2. Purchasing an Annuity: An annuity can provide a guaranteed income for life or for a set number of years.

3. Drawdown Schemes: These allow you to take a lump sum from your pension pot while the remainder continues to grow.

By planning prudently and investing wisely, retirement planning and pension schemes can secure your financial future, allowing you to enjoy the relaxation and opportunities that retirement brings. Plan well and you can look forward to your retirement as a time of financial independence and personal freedom.

Chapter 9. Risk Management and Insurance Strategies

In the domain of personal finance, how one manages risk plays an integral role in determining their eventual financial independence. Undeniably, insurance remains a vital component of any risk management strategy. Therefore, understanding the fundamentals of insurance and how it can be leveraged as a risk management tool is crucial. This chapter delves into risk management and insurance strategies in a bid to equip you with the requisite knowledge and make you adequately prepared for a financially secure future.

9.1. Insurance as a Risk Management Tool

Insurance plays a vital function in risk management by bringing about a transfer of financial risk. It shifts the risk of a considerable loss from you to the insurance company. Insurance, thus, provides a financial buffer against the unpredictable blows of fate that can render havoc on one's financial stability.

Be it your health, your life, your home or even your vehicle, insurance mitigates risk across various spheres of life. You pay a premium for this protection, and if a named peril transpires, resulting in financial loss, you can file an insurance claim to compensate for your loss. The nature of risk determines the type of insurance coverage chosen.

9.2. Types of Insurance

Several types of insurance policies can be included in a risk management strategy, and the ones you need depend upon your unique circumstances, lifestyle, and risk tolerance.

Life Insurance: This type of insurance important for anyone who has dependents. It generally pays out either on the death of the insured person or after a set period.

Health Insurance: With the rise in healthcare costs, health insurance becomes essential to cover potential medical expenses and protect against high medical bills.

Homeowner's or Renter's Insurance: Both insure against damage to your residence and protect against liability claims.

Auto Insurance: In most jurisdictions, this is legally necessary. It covers vehicular damage and liability as a result of an accident.

Disability Insurance: This type of insurance replaces a portion of your income if you become unable to work due to an illness or injury.

Long-term care Insurance: It covers the cost of personal care for a person with an extended physical illness, disability, or severe cognitive disorder.

Having bought the appropriate types of insurance, you must then consider the specific policies' details more closely.

9.3. Policies and Coverage

Every insurance policy has its specifics, and understanding these is indispensable to making the right choices. They can veer drastically, and for them to benefit you fully, you must ensure that every detail aligns with your needs and circumstances.

Take note of the insured amount, or the 'sum assured'. This is the amount that the insurer guarantees to pay upon the occurrence of the event insured against. Ensure this amount is sufficient to keep you financially stable in the event of a mishap.

Consider the premium - the amount payable annually to keep the policy active. Assess if the premium is affordable and aligns with your financial plan.

Also, check the policy term, the duration for which the policy is valid. In case of saving-based insurance policies, analyzing the maturity and death benefits is equally important.

Finally, check all inclusions and exclusions - what the policy covers, and what it does not. This will differ in different policies.

9.4. Risk Assessment and Insurance Need

The amount and type of insurance you need depends on the potential risks you may face. To conduct an effective risk assessment, consider potential life-altering events that may have a significant financial impact. Then analyze the likelihood of the event and its potential cost.

Then, keep in mind the concept of self-insurance. If you have enough saved to cover a potential risk yourself, you may not need insurance coverage for that risk. It's about balancing the cost, the risk, and the potential benefit and adopting a strategy that best suits your individual needs and circumstances.

9.5. Leveraging Insurance for Wealth Creation

Insurance doesn't just provide risk cover, it can also function as a tool for wealth creation. Certain policies, such as life insurance with a savings component or annuities, can act as investment vehicles.

In conclusion, managing risk is an ongoing and evolving task, needing continual reassessment as our circumstances, and the world around us, change. By understanding the potential risks, their potential impact, and by availing of the appropriate coverage, you can secure your journey towards financial independence. Insurance provides a safety net, protecting you against unforeseen calamities and ensuring that you remain on the path to a financially stable future.

Chapter 10. Tax Planning for Wealth Conservation

Understanding taxation is dramatically important because it plays a pivotal role in financial planning and wealth conservation. Proper tax planning can enable you to retain a significant part of your accumulated wealth and even expand it, instead of watching it diminish with taxation expenses. In this chapter, we will guide you through extensive strategies and methods of tax planning for long-term wealth conservation.

10.1. The Principles of Tax Planning

Before delving into strategies and plans, you must understand the foundational principles that underline tax planning. This will give you a better perspective on why certain tactics are practiced and advise you on the principles that should guide your decisions.

1. Be Proactive: Rather than waiting till the end of the financial year and rushing to reduce your tax liabilities, plan and act in advance. Plant your financial seeds early and watch them grow over time.

2. Lawfulness: Always ensure that your tax planning procedures comply with the tax laws of the land. Violations can lead to penalties and tarnish your financial reputation.

3. Diversification: Don't put all your eggs in one basket. Diversify your investments to benefit from various tax breaks associated with different investment avenues.

4. Understand Your Tax Bracket: Understand where you stand in terms of your income's tax liability. This will impact the type of tax-saving instruments that would be suitable for you.

10.2. Tax Efficient Investment Strategies

One of the primary ways to conserve wealth through tax planning is by making tax-efficient investment choices.

1. Consider Tax-Preferred Investments: Many countries encourage investment in certain sectors or funds through tax breaks. These can be in the form of tax-free income, tax deductions, or tax credits.

2. Use Tax-Advantaged Accounts: Consider using tax-advantaged accounts like the Roth IRA, Traditional IRA, or 401(k) in the USA. Similar provisions are made in other countries too. These usually fall into two categories — those that provide an immediate tax deduction but are taxable upon withdrawal, and those that do not provide an upfront deduction but grow tax-free and are tax-free upon retirement.

10.3. Strategies for Income Shifting

Income shifting refers to the process of transferring income from a higher-tax-rate taxpayer to a lower-one, legitimately. This could greatly reduce the amount of tax you're liable to pay.

1. Gifting: Transferring a portion of your wealth to a family member in a lower tax bracket can effectively reduce the amount of tax you pay. However, do be cautious of any gift-tax implications, if applicable.

2. Trusts: You can also shift income through trusts such as Grantor Retained Annuity Trusts (GRAT) and Charitable Remainder Trusts (CRT), amongst others.

10.4. Estate Planning for Wealth Preservation

Effective estate planning ensures that the maximum amount of wealth is left after paying the necessary taxes.

1. Utilize Estate Tax Exemptions: Many jurisdictions provide exemptions for a certain amount of estate value. It's crucial to plan your estate in a way that maximizes this exemption limit.

2. Irrevocable Life Insurance Trust (ILIT): An ILIT can provide liquidity to cover estate taxes, avoiding the need for a fire sale of assets.

Always remember, tax planning is not a one-time event but an ongoing process. The key to successful tax planning lies in constantly monitoring and adjusting your strategy to reflect changes in the tax laws and in your life. While this guide provides a robust outline for tax planning, it is essential to consult with a tax advisor to tailor an approach to your specific needs.

Chapter 11. Achieving and Sustaining Financial Independence

First and foremost, understanding the concept of financial independence is critical. It isn't merely about having extravagant wealth or the ability to purchase anything - it refers to the state of financial self-sufficiency where you can live comfortably without having to work intensively.

11.1. The Fundamental Steps

There are five crucial steps you need to follow to achieve financial independence no matter from what stage you start:

1. Assess Your Current Financial Status

2. Define Your Financial Goals

3. Formulate a Detailed Financial Plan

4. Take Action

5. Regularly Review and Adjust Your Plan

11.2. Assess Your Current Financial Status

Accurately assessing your current financial status is a mandatory starting point. You must have a clear understanding of where you are to plan how to get where you want to go.

To avoid doubts or red herrings, you need to assess to the last detail. Determine your net worth by subtracting your total liabilities from your total assets. Record all your income streams: primary, secondary, and even those little extras that occasionally come in. Don't forget about your expenditures: recurrent bills, food, transport, fuel, etc.

With the total picture in sight, you can then move to the next stage.

11.3. Define Your Financial Goals

Financial independence will mean different things to different people. For some, it may be to retire at 50 with a comfortable pension. For others, it might be scaling a business to a point where it can smoothly run without their daily input.

Your goals need to be specific, measurable, achievable, relevant, and time-bound (SMART).

For example, "I want to retire at age 50 with a net worth of $500,000, and for this to happen, I need to save or invest $10,000 every year for the next 20 years."

11.4. Formulate a Detailed Financial Plan

A detailed financial plan is your roadmap to financial independence. It outlines how you propose to get from your current status to where you intend to be.

A robust financial plan should feature your budget, savings plan, debt repayment plan, and investment plan.

Your debt repayment plan needs to highlight how much you owe, to whom, the interest rates, monthly minimum payments, and a strategy for clearing these debts.

11.5. Take Action

Without action, your financial plan is merely a wish list.

Whether it's getting started with a savings plan, buying stocks or bonds, reducing your expenditures, or starting a side hustle, take the first steps, no matter how small they seem. The journey to financial independence is not a sprint; it's a steady marathon.

Remember, the best time to get started is now.

11.6. Regularly Review and Adjust Your Plan

It's crucial not to develop a "set it and forget it" mindset after creating your plan. Your financial circumstances will undoubtedly change over time, and so too should your budget, savings, and investment plans.

A financial plan is not static; it should adapt in response to shifts in income streams, expenditure, financial goals, and market conditions. As such, make a habit of checking in on your plan and making tweaks where necessary every quarter or semi-annually.

11.7. Building an Emergency Fund

One of the hallmarks of a financially independent individual is a healthy emergency fund. This is a rainy-day fund you can fall back on when life throws you a financial curveball.

A recommended starting point is to have three to six months' worth of living expenses set aside in a separate, highly liquid savings or money market account.

11.8. Effective Budgeting

Budgeting is a critical tool in your journey to financial independence. It helps you make the most out of your income and savings by encouraging financial discipline.

It works best when you allocate roles to every dollar in your possession, preferably ahead of time. This way, you have a clear-cut plan on how to spend, instead of being forced into spontaneous, sometimes regrettable, financial decisions.

11.9. Debt Management

Debt is the direct opposite of financial independence. While some debts, like mortgages and student loans, may be inevitable, it's essential to have a focused plan on becoming debt-free.

Pay off high-interest debts first, carry out a balance transfer to lower-rate cards where possible, consider debt consolidation, or seek professional financial counselling. Adopt effective strategies that can yield huge benefits.

11.10. Investment Strategies

Investment is the only sure pathway to growing your wealth over time. Whether it's stocks, bonds, mutual funds, real estate, investing in a business or buying valuables such as art and jewelry, the fundamental rule remains: buy low, sell high.

11.11. Conclusion

Achieving financial independence is indeed a journey, one filled with its challenges and victories. The freedom that comes with it is worth all the conscientious planning, disciplined spending, and calculated investing. Forging ahead, always remember the goal and let it be the motivation that keeps you on track.

www.ingramcontent.com/pod-product-compliance
Lightning Source LLC
Chambersburg PA
CBHW071044260726
48661CB00007B/3142